Moo-rry Cl...

The Murrays

The Famous Jersey Cow
MERRY MAIDEN and her Calf
Hoods Animal Statuettes   owned at HOOD FARM Lowell, Mass.
Copyright 1905 by C.I. Hood & Co.

OVER

THE COW COLLECTION

Edited by
Susan Fortunato
and Giema Tsakuginow

LONGMEADOW PRESS

We gratefully appreciate the following artists and representatives for letting us use their work: Barbara Wallace, Gay Bumgarner, Susan Leopold, Art Curtis, Peggy Tagel, Bob Jones, Paul Lackner, Stockworks, Allford Trotman Associates, Dulong and Woods, Inc., Country Crafts & More, Artworks, and McVay's Old Wood Creations.

Copyright © 1992 by Longmeadow Press

Cover design by Barbara Cohen Aronica and Jan Halper Scaglia
Interior design by Barbara Cohen Aronica

ISBN: 0-681-41572-X
Printed in Singapore
First Edition
0 9 8 7 6 5 4 3 2 1

Acknowledgments

I am grateful for the assistance and good sense of humor of the people at Longmeadow Press: Adrienne Ingrum, Mark Slavinsky, and especially my editor, Pam Altschul.

There were many new friends who helped me as well. Maribeth Carey at Storey Communications provided me with invaluable assistance; the great people at *Holy Cow* and Hope Cox and Nancy Black from *Everything Cows* made the afternoons of research go by quickly. Special thanks goes to my son, Graham, for his consistently long, uninterrupted naps.

—s.f.

Cows are my passion.

—Charles Dickens

Cows represent the family farm more than any other animal. But I think the cow represents motherhood. Governor William Hoard of Wisconsin, who served around the turn of the century, had a sign posted on the door of his barn that read:

> *Remember that this is the Home of Mother.*
> *Treat each cow as a mother should be treated.*

When we pass by cows grazing in a meadow, we invariably turn to stare. Maybe this is because the mild cow leads an idyllic life placidly chewing her cud, having babies, and generally living a life of pleasant distractions.

Not so long ago most American families lived and worked on small farms. Even as they began to migrate toward towns and cities, they almost always brought their cow.

Over time, cows have become an important part of the American myth—they represent the wholesomeness and serenity of a generation long gone.

When we surround ourselves with cow memorabilia, we are reaffirming our belief in the pioneer spirit that helped to forge a nation. We are saying yes to idealism and patriotism. Yes to whole milk and yogurt.

The Cow's Story: A Short History of Cows

You do de pullin', Sis Cow, en I'll do de gruntin'.

–Joel Chandler Harris, Uncle Remus and Friends

In almost every ancient civilization, there is some history
of milk cows. From the ruins of a temple near Babylon
that show 6,000-year-old depictions of men milking cows,
to Sanskrit that refers to milk as one of the essential foods,
it is indisputable that cows have developed right
alongside people.

Hindu Cows

In ancient Sanskrit literature, the cow world is considered the highest and greatest of all worlds. Surabhi (the cow of abundance) came down from the world of cows and implored Krishna to ensure the happiness of cows and well-meaning people. Indeed, Mohandas Gandhi considered cow protection one of the most important social issues, stating, "To protect her is to protect all the dumb creatures of God's creation."

In prehistoric times, butter was "churned" by placing cream in a skin bag and tying it to a horse or camel. The movement of the animal produced the butter.

The first documentation of butter occurs in the Vedic hymns of India written about 2000–3000 B.C. Hindus valued their cows by the quantity of butter they could produce from their cow's milk. The ancient Greeks and Romans prized butter as a medicine, hair gel, and ointment.

Moo-ments in History

350 B.C.   Aristotle reported that cows in Greece gave 32 quarts of milk a day.

1st century   Pliny claims that a thousand–pound cheese wheels were produced in the Po valley.

1004 A.D.   The Vikings brought the first cows to the New World.

1493   Columbus brought cows on his second voyage to America.

1611   Cows were imported to Jamestown, VA.

1624   Cows were brought to the Plymouth Colony.

1848   The ice cream freezer was granted a U.S. patent.

1857   Pasteurization was discovered.

1874	Robert M. Green invented the Ice-Cream Soda.
1881	Ed Berner of Two Rivers, Wisconsin, created the ice-cream sundae when he poured chocolate sauce on vanilla ice cream.
1904	The Ice-Cream Cone debuted at the St. Louis World's Fair.
1915	The National Dairy Council was founded.
1919	Chocolate milk was introduced.
1937	The first June Dairy Month was celebrated.
1964	Plastic milk containers were introduced.
1987	A Dairy Complex, complete with a real dairy barn, was opened at the Milwaukee County Zoo.

A Beginner's Guide to Breeds, Cowbells, & Proverbs

Whether you aspire to milk your own cow someday or would just like to ask with some authority for that Holstein–patterned cap, you'll need some basic facts at your fingertips, so you don't *udderly* embarrass yourself.

Cattle Calls

Males are **bulls**. Females are **heifers** until they give birth, and then they are **cows**. Young cattle are **calves**.

  In Europe there are between forty and fifty breeds of cows, so we are especially blessed in the United States to have only six major dairy breeds:

Ayrshire These plucky cows originated from Scotland and are bright red and white or nearly all white with small patches of red.

Brown Swiss One of the largest and hardiest of all dairy breeds, Brown Swiss are dark brown with black horn tips.

Holstein The Dutch brought Holsteins with them when they settled in New Amsterdam (now New York) in 1630. Their distinctive black and white markings symbolize to many of us what cow loving is all about.

Guernsey The color of the Guernsey ranges from fawn to almost red with white patches, especially around the legs and belly. Its milk is a distinctive yellow color.

Jersey Although usually associated with a fawn or light brown color, the Jersey can also be cream or black and have varying white patches. The Jersey is one of the smallest dairy cows.

Shorthorn First brought to America in 1783, these cows have a distinctive, red-and-white or roan coloring.

I never saw a purple cow—
    I never hope to see one:
But I can tell you anyhow,
    I'd rather see then be one.

—Gelett Burgess

Sometimes, fame can be a cruel muse:

Ah, yes, I wrote "The Purple Cow"
    I'm sorry now I wrote it!
But I can tell you anyhow
    I'll kill you if you quote it.

—Gelett Burgess

A cow's normal temperature is 101.5 degrees Fahrenheit.

❖

A cow's age is based on the age at which she is calved.

❖

Irish farmers say "God bless" and spit three times when a calf is born.

❖

Milk is mentioned 44 times in the Old Testament.

❖

An average cow has more than 40,000 jaw movements a day.

Cow Bells

Although cowbells are sometimes thought of as a decorator
touch to a sun room, they still have practical use on the
farm. Most importantly, they are used to keep track
of the family cow which is still often allowed to roam
freely. They are also used to help timid cows assert
themselves at the feeding trough.

The friendly cow all red and white,
    I love with all my heart:
She gives me cream with all her might,
    To eat with apple tart.

—*Robert Louis Stevenson*

Social Cows

Cows are by nature social animals and are not fond of being alone. In fact, if there are no calves or cows nearby, cows will make friends with people, horses, or dogs!

We milk the cow of the world, and as we do,
We whisper in her ear, "You are not true."

—Richard Wilbur

Let the woman into Paradise, she'll bring her cow along.

—Russian Proverb

Kiss till the cow comes home.

—*Beaumont and Fletcher*

Every beast of the forest is mine,
and the cattle upon a thousand hills.

—Psalms 50:10

High diddle diddle
The cat and the fiddle,
The cow jumped over the moon;
The little dog laughed
To see such a craft
And the dish ran away with the spoon.

Cow Americana

There is no way of knowing precisely how people began keeping cows, but one of the most popular theories is that a hunter killed a cow and took the baby home to raise. In fact, the first domesticated cows were probably runts. Soon the number of cows you kept, regardless of their size, became an almost universal way of gauging your wealth. The Latin words *pecunia*, meaning money, and *pecus*, meaning cow, are as closely related as the two concepts were in ancient Rome. Even today, some African tribes still use this method of calculating wealth.

Americans are particularly particular about their famous, and not so famous cows.

Mrs. O'Leary's Cow

Poor Mrs. O'Leary's cow. Poor Mrs. O'Leary. On a
fall night in Chicago in 1871, Mrs. O'Leary's cow
kicked over a lantern. Three days later, after the largest
fire ever to engulf an American city, over 17,000
buildings had burned to the ground.

Elsie the Cow

The Borden Company introduced Elsie the Cow as a cartoon character in the thirties, but it was really during the 1939 World's Fair that Elsie became an international spokescow. In fact, Elsie had become so popular as a cartoon that a special "boudoir" was designed for her at the World's Fair exhibit apart from the other cows.

Soon her husband, Elmer, and daughter, Beulah, joined her in the exhibit. When Elsie was asked to appear in the movie *Little Men*, starring Jack Oakie and Kay Francis, the exhibit was temporarily changed to the home of a bachelor father. When Elsie returned, it was Elmer who got his big break, appearing on a bottle of glue that the Borden Company made in 1947. Elsie had her second child, a boy, and a contest was held to pick his name. Beauregard joined his mother on publicity tours.

In the sixties, there was an attempt to replace Elsie as the symbol for Borden milk, but the public protested, and Elsie was brought back for a triumphant tour in 1971. She has opened the Ice Cream Parlor in Disneyworld and appeared in the Tournament of Roses Parade.

Enola Gay

Paul Tibbets, the pilot of the B–29 that dropped
the first atomic bomb over Hiroshima, Japan,
named his bomber after his family's cow.

Top 5 Cows in Advertising

1. Elsie the Cow

2. La Vache Qui Rit: The Laughing Cow

3. The Ben & Jerry's Ice Cream cows

4. Chex cereal cows: "Don't put a cow out of work. Eat Chex with milk."

5. Lea & Perrins: "The steak sauce only a cow could hate."

Cow Spots

Stores

California
Udderly Perfect
1201 Highland Avenue
Manhattan Beach, CA 90266
(310) 546-5322

Florida
Udderly Country
124 W. Pine Street, Suite 110
Orlando, FL 32801
(407) 843-2697

Illinois
Spotted Cow
4600 N. Prospect Road
Peoria, Illinois 61614
(309) 682-8120

Vermont
Everything Cows, The Cow Place
Main Street
Stowe, Vermont 05672
(802) 253-8779

Virginia
The Spotted Cow, Ltd.
1985 Landstown
Virginia Beach,VA 23456
(804) 427-9483

Cowtalogs

Everything Cows
P.O. Box 1019
Stowe, Vermont 05672

Woody Jackson's Holy Cow, Inc.
52 Seymour Street
 P.O. Box 906
Middlebury, VT 05753
(800) 543-COWS

Cow Art
River Hills, Wisconsin

Three polyester cow sculptures are on exhibit at the Bradley Sculpture Garden. They are the work of swedish sculptor Samuel Bari.

Cow Decorator
Mark Epstein

Hope Cox and Nancy Black, the owners of Everything Cows, got so many requests for bovine decorating tips that they decided to expand to include a decorating department. New York designer Mark Epstein will come to your home and spread a little cattle cheer!

Cowtown Festival
New Holstein, Wisconsin

This hamlet is known throughout Wisconsin for sponsoring this festival which annually offers a car show, dance, sidewalk sales and the Cowtown race.

Darcy Rent-A-Cow
Watertown, Wisconsin

Just not ready to make a commitment? Well, call Rent-a-Cow and they can provide you with a Holstein of just about any age. The cost is about $30-35 a month and you keep all the milk and calves.

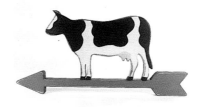

The Cow Book
Storey Communications

The Family Cow, by Dirk can Loon, is the finest book I've found for helping both the novice and experienced farm person with the daily routine of keeping a cow.

■ 45 ■